D1263262

PHILADELPHIA EAGLES

BY BARRY WILNER

The Child's World®

Published by The Child's World®
1980 Lookout Drive • Mankato, MN 56003-1705
800-599-READ • www.childsworld.com

Acknowledgments
The Child's World®: Mary Berendes, Publishing Director
Red Line Editorial: Editorial direction
The Design Lab: Design
Amnet: Production

Design Element: Dean Bertoncelj/Shutterstock Images
Photographs ©: Damian Strohmeyer/AP Images, cover;
Matt Rourke/AP Images, 5; John Biever/Icon Sportswire,
7; NFL/AP Images, 9, 19, 29; Evan Pinkus/AP Images, 11;
Shutterstock Images, 13; Aspen Photo/Shutterstock Images,
14–15; Pro Football Hall of Fame/AP Images, 17; Brian
Garfinkel/AP Images, 21; Amy Sancetta/AP Images, 23;
Michael Perez/AP Images, 25; Tom DiPace/AP Images, 27

ISBN 9781634070058
LCCN 2014959710

Printed in the United States of America
Mankato, MN
July, 2015
PAO2265

ABOUT THE AUTHOR

Barry Wilner has written 41 books, including many for young readers. He is a sports writer for The Associated Press and has covered such events as the Super Bowl, Olympics, and World Cup. He lives in Garnerville, New York.

TABLE OF CONTENTS

GO, EAGLES!

Bert Bell and Lud Wray wanted to bring a football team to Philadelphia. In 1933, they bought the rights to the Frankford Yellow Jackets for $25,000. They renamed the team the Eagles. They lost their first game 56-0. But the Eagles were here to stay. In 1939, they played in the first professional football game on TV. Philadelphia fans have stayed loyal even when the team was losing. Let's meet the Eagles.

Tight end Zach Ertz fights for yardage in a game against the Seattle Seahawks on December 7, 2014.

WHO ARE THE EAGLES?

The Philadelphia Eagles play in the National Football **League** (NFL). They are one of the 32 teams in the NFL. The NFL includes the American Football Conference (AFC) and the National Football Conference (NFC). The winner of the NFC plays the winner of the AFC in the Super Bowl. The Eagles play in the East Division of the NFC. They have played in the big game twice. They lost both times. Philadelphia won three NFL Championships before the Super Bowl began after the 1966 season.

Quarterback Donovan McNabb led the Eagles to a Super Bowl appearance after the 2004 season.

WHERE THEY CAME FROM

The Eagles were named by owner Bert Bell. He thought the team would soar. But the Eagles started with ten losing seasons. They finally had a winning season in 1943. That year, many players were fighting in World War II. So the Eagles combined with the Pittsburgh Steelers for one season. They were called the Steagles. The Eagles won their third NFL Championship in 1960. But they made the playoffs just four times in the next 27 years.

Halfback Ted Dean (35) runs with the ball in Philadelphia's 17-13 win over the Green Bay Packers in the NFL Championship Game on December 26, 1960.

WHO THEY PLAY

The Philadelphia Eagles play 16 games each season. With so few games, each one is important. Every year, the Eagles play two games against each of the other three teams in their division. Those teams are the New York Giants, Washington Redskins, and Dallas Cowboys. The Eagles also play six other teams from the NFC and four from the AFC. The Giants and Eagles are big **rivals**. They have played each other at least twice every year except 1967, 1969, and 1982. New York is 100 miles from Philadelphia. That means fans of both teams can easily go to games.

Fans of both teams love it when the Eagles and Giants meet on the football field.

WHERE THEY PLAY

The Eagles have played in six stadiums in Philadelphia. They have shared with baseball and football teams. These days, they call Lincoln Financial Field home. The stadium opened in 2003. The Eagles share "the Linc" with the Temple University football team. Soccer games are played there, too. More than 69,000 fans fit in the stadium.

The Eagles lost 17–0 to the Tampa Bay Buccaneers on September 8, 2003, in the first regular season game at Lincoln Financial Field.

THE FOOTBALL FIELD

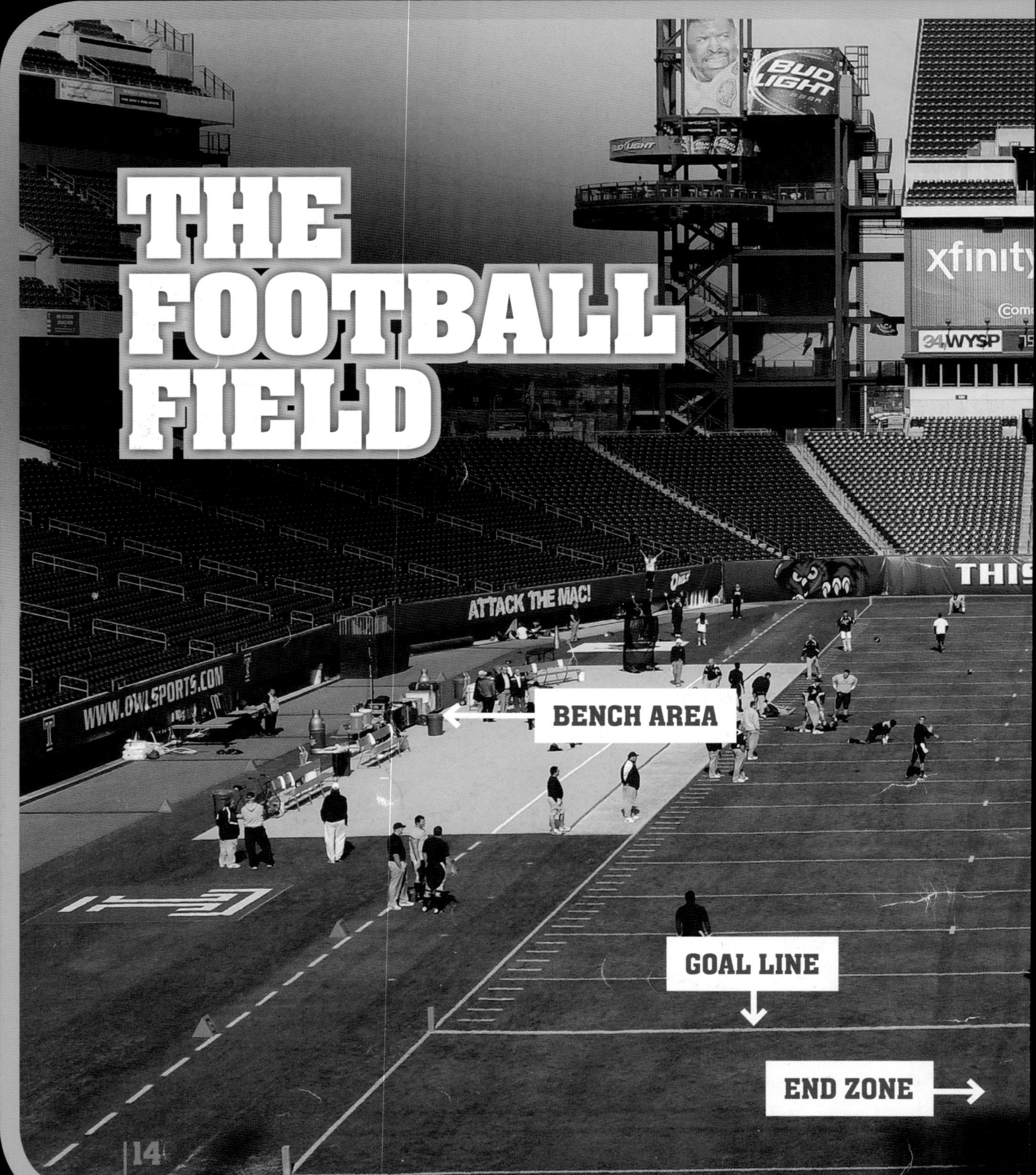

BENCH AREA

GOAL LINE

END ZONE →

GOAL POST

SIDELINE

HASH MARKS

20-YARD LINE

BIG DAYS

The Eagles have had some great moments in their history. Here are three of the greatest:

1948—The Eagles won their first championship. They played the Chicago Cardinals on December 19. There was a snowstorm in Philadelphia. That was good for the Eagles' strong defense. Halfback Steve Van Buren scored the only **touchdown** to win "The Blizzard Bowl" 7-0.

1978—It was November 19. The Eagles trailed the New York Giants 17-12 in Giants Stadium. There was less than a minute left. But New York quarterback Joe Pisarcik **fumbled**. Philadelphia cornerback Herm Edwards picked up the ball and scored. The Eagles won 19-17 in "The Miracle at the Meadowlands."

Halfback Steve Van Buren (15) scores the winning touchdown in "The Blizzard Bowl."

2004—Philadelphia had lost three NFC Championship Games in a row. But the Eagles beat the Atlanta Falcons 27-10 on January 23, 2005. That sent the Eagles to the Super Bowl. Philadelphia was hit with bad weather that weekend. Still, thousands of fans celebrated in the streets.

TOUGH DAYS

Football is a hard game. Even the best teams have rough games and seasons. Here are some of the toughest times in Eagles history:

1936—The season started with a win. But then the Eagles lost 11 games in a row. That included six **shutouts**. Philadelphia scored just 51 points all season.

1992—Eagles defensive lineman Jerome Brown died on June 25, 1992. He was killed in a car accident. The team and its fans were very sad. Philadelphia retired his jersey, No. 99. That means no other Eagles player can wear it.

2012—Andy Reid is the most successful Eagles coach ever. He won 140 games, including 10 in the playoffs,

A player at the Pro Bowl on February 7, 1993, honors Jerome Brown by writing Brown's jersey No. 99 on shoe tape.

and six division titles. But the team went 4-12 under him this season. The Eagles lost 11 of their final 12 games. Reid was fired at the end of the season.

MEET THE FANS

Philadelphia's team song is "Fly Eagles Fly." It used to be called "The Eagles' Victory Song" before the words were changed. Fans sing it before home games. They also sing when Philadelphia scores touchdowns. Fans like to meet up before games to **tailgate**. They enjoy sharing their love of the Eagles. Team mascot Swoop gets the crowd fired up.

Eagles mascot Swoop leads the team out for its game against the Kansas City Chiefs on September 19, 2013.

HEROES THEN

Chuck Bednarik played center and linebacker. He was super tough. He played from 1949 to 1962 and made eight **Pro Bowls**. Defensive lineman Reggie White is one of the best pass rushers ever. His nickname was "The Minister of Defense." That is because he was a church minister. White spent eight seasons with the Eagles. He led the NFL in **sacks** twice. Donovan McNabb was the team's starting quarterback from 2000 to 2009. The Eagles made the playoffs eight of those ten years.

n Marino

21

Eagles defensive end Reggie White sacks Miami Dolphins quarterback Da
on December 13, 1987.

22

HEROES NOW

L inebacker Connor Barwin joined Philadelphia in 2013. He is a hard-working player. He had 14.5 sacks in 2014. That was fourth in the NFL. Barwin made his first Pro Bowl that year. Mychal Kendricks is another Eagles linebacker. He had three interceptions and four fumble recoveries in 2013. Star running back DeMarco Murray left the Dallas Cowboys for the Eagles in 2015. He led the league in rushing in 2014. Wide receiver Jordan Matthews gets fans excited. He was a rookie in 2014. He had eight touchdowns that season.

Wide receiver Jordan Matthews catches a pass in a game against the Washington Redskins on September 21, 2014.

GEARING UP

NFL players wear team uniforms. They wear helmets and pads to keep them safe. Cleats help them make quick moves and run fast. Some players wear extra gear for protection.

THE FOOTBALL

NFL footballs are made of leather. Under the leather is a lining that fills with air to give the ball its shape. The leather has bumps or "pebbles." These help players grip the ball. Laces help players control their throws. Footballs are also called "pigskins" because some of the first balls were made from pig bladders. Today they are made of leather from cows.

Wide receiver Jeremy Maclin missed the entire 2013 season with a knee injury.

HELMET

SHOULDER PADS

GLOVES

THIGH PADS

FOOTBALL

CLEATS

SPORTS STATS

 Here are some of the all-time career records for the Eagles. All the stats are through the 2014 season.

PASSING YARDS

Donovan McNabb 32,873

Ron Jaworski 26,963

RUSHING YARDS

LeSean McCoy 6,792

Wilbert Montgomery 6,538

RECEPTIONS

Harold Carmichael 589

Pete Retzlaff 452

INTERCEPTIONS

Eric Allen, Bill Bradley, and Brian Dawkins 34

SACKS

Reggie White 124

Trent Cole 85.5

POINTS

David Akers 1,323

Bobby Walston 881

Wide receiver Harold Carmichael finished in the top 10 in the NFL in receiving touchdowns in 8 of his 13 seasons with the Eagles.

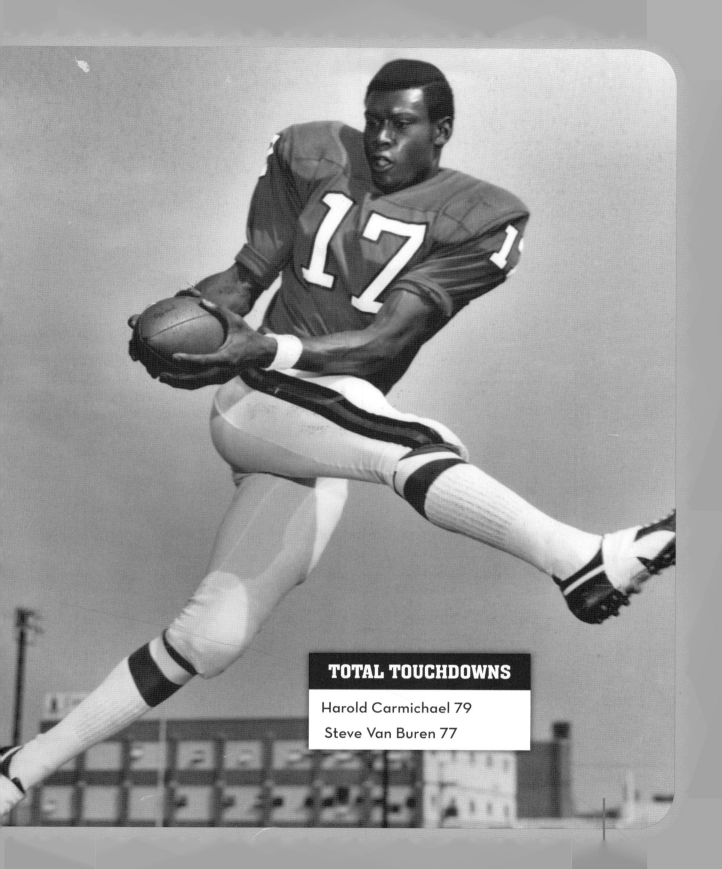

TOTAL TOUCHDOWNS

Harold Carmichael 79

Steve Van Buren 77

GLOSSARY

fumbled when a player lost control of the football and the other team got it

league an organization of sports teams that compete against each other

Pro Bowls the NFL's All-Star game where the best players in the league compete

rivals teams whose games bring out the greatest emotion between the players and the fans on both sides

sacks when the quarterback is tackled behind the line of scrimmage before he can throw the ball

shutouts when a team scores zero points

tailgate when fans gather outside of the stadium before a game to picnic around their vehicles

touchdown a play in which the ball is held in the other team's end zone, resulting in six points

FIND OUT MORE

IN THE LIBRARY

Gordon, Bob. *Game Of My Life: Philadelphia Eagles*. New York: Skyhorse, 2013.

Stewart, Mark. *Team Spirit: The Philadelphia Eagles*. Chicago: Norwood House Press, 2012.

Wyner, Zach. *Inside The NFL: The Philadelphia Eagles*. New York: Av2, 2014.

ON THE WEB

Visit our Web site for links about the Philadelphia Eagles:
childsworld.com/links

Note to Parents, Teachers, and Librarians: We routinely verify our Web links to make sure they are safe and active sites. So encourage your readers to check them out!

INDEX